W9-CGS-259

Minute Motivators for Men

Stan Toler

08 07 06 05 04   10 9 8 7 6 5 4 3 2 1

Minute Motivators for Men
ISBN 978-0-9824906-3-1

Copyright © 2004, 2011
Dust Jacket Press
PO Box 721243
Oklahoma City, OK 73172
www.dustjacket.com <http://www.dustjacket.com>
800-495-0192

Printed in the United States of America. All rights reserved
under International Copyright Law. Contents and/or cover
may not be reproduced in whole or in part in any form
without th eexpress written consent of the Publisher.

Unless otherwise indicated, all Scripture quotations are from the
Holy Bible, New International Version® (NIV®), Copyright
© 1973, 1978, 1984 International Bible Society. Used by
permission of Zondervan. All rights reserved.

Contents

Introduction

A few good men? No, there are millions of them—in your world, in your community, all around you. Everywhere, there are men who have decided to live above the trends and the times. These men are more interested in making a difference than in making a million. They refuse to trade principle for power, love for lust, or compassion for a promotion.

How do they do it? They follow the game plan. They make the moves that other winners have made. They make the right choices. They live by the most important standard—excellence.

Minute Motivators for Men is a playbook. Paragraph by paragraph, sentence by sentence, this book will give you the insights that will put you in scoring position.

On to victory!

Stan Toler

Take charge of your attitude.

The greatest discovery of my generation is that man can alter his life simply by altering his attitude of mind.

—William James

ATTITUDE

There are many things you can't control. You can't control the weather, the traffic, the actions of your boss, or the outcome of a sporting event. But there is one thing you can control: your attitude.

You can't control the weather, but you can choose to sing in the rain. You are in command of your own actions and reactions. You choose whether to become angry or remain calm, whether to be upbeat or negative. Take charge of your mental attitude. You can load up on the negative and harmful, or you can put a filter on your thoughts. It's up to you.

Choose to be a positive thinker. There's a "partly sunny" in every single day. The sun is shining behind the clouds. Look for some rays.

Make it a habit to look for the best instead of the worst, wear a smile, and give the other guy a break. It's your life, after all. Take charge of it!

What you think, you are.

Make everyone feel important.

There is nothing better
than the encouragement
of a good friend.

—Katharine Butler Hathaway

ENCOURAGEMENT

Show me a person who doesn't like to be encouraged, and I'll show you a person who doesn't like anything. All the people in your life—from wives, to kids, to in-laws, to coworkers—have this in common: They need encouragement.

Here's a secret to success in life: put other people ahead of yourself. Make other people feel valued. Offer your chair to a newcomer and be liberal with pats on the back. Say "Good job!" easily and often. When you encourage others, they'll join your team. Together, you'll accomplish more than you ever could alone.

How do you become an encourager? It's simple. Think of other people first. You don't always have to be first in line. Someone you know needs a pat on the back, rather than a kick in the seat of the pants. Someone may need recognition far more than you—perhaps someone who has always been told they were inferior. You can be a change agent.

Learn to put yourself in second place, and other people will think you're number one.

Plan time alone.

Search me, O God, and know

my heart; test me and

know my anxious thoughts.

—Psalm 139:23

INTROSPECTION

There's a very important person in your life, someone you should get to know. This person has great influence over you—more than your friends, your family, or your associates. Who is it? It's you.

Develop the habit of spending time alone for introspection. A few minutes a day of inward reflection will develop your outer character. As you think about what you do, how you respond to situations, the emotions you feel, and why you feel them, you'll get to know yourself. That knowledge will be valuable as you cope with life, especially in a crisis.

Take a few minutes at the end of the day to reflect on what you think, how you feel, and who you are. Or block off a little time during your lunch break to sit quietly and just think.

Wasted time? Hardly. It may be the most important time slot in your daily schedule.

A few minutes spent staring out the window may give you a good look into your soul.

Extend a helping hand.

We really do need each other.

—Rueben Welch

BROTHERHOOD

We're in this together. If you and I are going to prosper in our communities and in our careers, we'll need to depend upon each other.

Relying on others ought to come naturally, but it doesn't. Human beings are too used to seeing one another as the enemy. We compete with each other for jobs, promotions, good grades—you name it. It's tempting to look only at our differences and see one another as strangers.

We're not, really. We sons of Adam are more alike than we are different. Sure, we may have a different skin color or speak different languages. But we share common needs for friendship, peace, and security.

Begin to see yourself as part of a fraternity—not one that's known by some Greek letters, but one that includes all men everywhere. Look at your next-door neighbor as a member of your team. Look for ways to work together. Exchange a handshake with that coworker who is difficult to get along with. He's facing some of the same problems you are. Most importantly, look for ways to join hands with the men in your church.

Imagine what you might accomplish if you join forces and work together.

Be bold in what you stand for.

One man with courage
makes a majority.

—Andrew Jackson

COURAGE

That old saying is really true: If you don't stand for something, you'll fall for anything. Be a person who has strong values, and then stick to those values.

Courage isn't something you see only in Bruce Willis movies. It's a down-to-earth virtue that men need in order to be good husbands, fathers, and citizens. If you believe in something, sooner or later that belief will be challenged. That's where courage comes in.

Courage is telling the truth when company profits are on the line.

Courage is providing for your family by going to work every day, even when you don't feel like going.

Courage is raising positive kids in a negative world.

Courage is being a man of God in a world that scoffs at faith and values.

Courage is standing for what's right, even when it's not popular.

Who is the most courageous man I know? He's the guy who lives his faith, no matter what. He's a hero in my book.

You are what you stand for.

Don't be afraid to take a risk.

Man is so made that whenever anything fires his soul, impossibilities vanish.

—LaFontaine

DETERMINATION

Edmund Hillary was a bookkeeper from Auckland, New Zealand. But then he decided to take a risk. On May 29, 1953, he became the first man to set foot on the summit of Mount Everest. Sir Edmund Hillary stepped out of the accounting room and into the pages of history because he was willing to take a risk.

No good thing in your life will happen on its own. If you want any positive change, you must be willing to step out from where you are and move toward it.

Are you willing to leave the security of a weekly paycheck to start your own business venture?

Are you willing to risk rejection by asking for a date?

Are you willing to force your way past a pile of "I told you so's" to make one more crack at reforming your behavior?

You may have to surrender something good in order to gain something better in your life. As someone once said, "you can't make a good omelet without breaking a few eggs."

Laugh easily.

The human race has one
really effective weapon,
and that is laughter.

—Mark Twain

LAUGHTER

"Laugh, and the world laughs with you," according to Ella Wheeler Wilcox. She was right. When you don a smile, you'll have plenty of company.

Laughter is good for you in several ways. It's good for your heart, literally, to laugh once in a while. A good sense of humor improves your physical health.

Laughter is good for your emotional health as well. Humor is a great stress buster. When you're so upset you don't know whether to laugh or cry, choose laughter every time.

Laughter is good for your social life. Would you rather be around someone who obviously enjoys life or someone who is merely enduring it?

Laughter benefits you in a spiritual way also. When you can laugh at yourself, and don't take yourself too seriously, you're one step closer to true humility. So go ahead and laugh out loud. It'll do you good.

The laugh you hold in may be your groan.

Face challenges head on.

Confidence is the first requisite
to great undertakings.

—Samuel Johnson

CONFIDENCE

There are two types of people in this world: those who ignore their problems and those who tackle them head on. Not surprisingly, the difference correlates directly with those who fail and those who succeed.

People who ignore problems usually wind up with bigger problems. Small office problems become staff revolts. Tiny pinging sounds become blown engines. Little warning signs become full-blown heart attacks.

People who face challenges head on are problem solvers. They get to the root of the problem quickly and keep their lives, and the lives of those around them, running smoothly. They make necessary adjustments now instead of later.

What does it take to be a problem solver? First, one needs the confidence that the future will be better than the past. Second, one must admit that the cause is worthy of the effect.

Make this inner determination today: "With God's help, I am able to handle any problem that comes my way."

Stand on that rock, and you will be taller than your challenge.

Remember, failure is not fatal.

Failure is delay, but not defeat.

It is a temporary detour,

not a dead-end street.

—Willaim Arthur Ward

FAILURE

The fighter who falls down is not defeated. It's the fighter who doesn't get up who loses the match. The ballplayer who fakes a limp doesn't win; the winner is the one who plays with pain.

Understand this: you *will* fail. But failure is not fatal, as long as you recover from it.

Everybody fails in life. We make mistakes in judgment; we become careless or selfish. Sometimes we just plain blow it. These things happen.

Your life will never be judged by the day of your greatest failure, but by the day after. What did you do next? What adjustments did you make in your game plan?

If you learn from failure, you grow.

If you become determined through failure, you succeed.

If you are angered by failure, you're motivated to change.

If you rise from failure, you go on to greater things.

Have you messed it up somewhere along the way? Welcome to the club. The critical question is "What are you going to do next?"

Think creatively.

Imagination is more
important than knowledge.

—Albert Einstein

CREATIVITY

There's a myth in our culture, which holds that women are more creative than men—and most men believe it. For whatever reason, many men have swallowed this fish story and believe that their role in life is to plod along, cutting the grass, fixing the cars, and cleaning the garage without ever having an original, daring, creative thought.

Baloney.

Hidden inside your brain is a fountain of creative energy. Find it, draw from it, and let the creativity flow. That energy might include music or the arts—two areas in which creativity is useful. But it might include more common pursuits like your career, your home, and even your finances.

Have you hit the glass ceiling at work? Look for creative ways to increase your effectiveness—or better yet, find a new position where you can grow.

Is your home no longer adequate for your growing family? Brainstorm ways to make the most of your space or make low-cost renovations.

Could you use additional income? There are money-making possibilities right under you nose—if you'll be creative in looking for them.

Be willing to change.

When you're through changing,
you're through.

—Bruce Barton

CHANGE

If all you are willing to do is what you are doing, then all you will ever be is what you are. If you are unwilling to think, grow, learn, and change, then it will be impossible for you to achieve anything beyond what you now see. However, if you are willing to make some changes, the possibilities are limitless.

What is your greatest dream or desire in life? Do you want to earn more money? Get married? Put your kids through college? Be healthier?

Now, what are you willing to do in order to make that happen? Chances are, accomplishing these goals will require change in your life. You might need to continue your education in order to get a better job; change your lifestyle in order get along well in a relationship; or change your eating habits in order to improve your health. You'll certainly have to change something if you want to grow.

Where do you want to be, and what are you willing to change in order to get there? Change makes more "cents."

Be a part of the solution.

Every problem contains the
seeds of its own solution.

—Stanley Arnold

PROBLEMS

You've seen them. They exist in every office, on every team, on every work crew. They're the naysayers—the people who see nothing but problems and often are the cause of them. They're morale busters. They're confidence killers. They're the guys who are always saying that it can't be done. They don't "bump and run" like a skilled racecar driver; they just bump.

Make up your mind never to join them. Determine that you will be part of the solution, not part of the problem. Determine to be a fixer, not a wrecker.

When the supply chain breaks down, don't gripe. Ask, "What can we do to help?"

When the management team comes out with a new idea, don't shoot it down. Ask thoughtful questions, and then get on board.

When sales are down, don't blame the economy, the marketing team, or the product. Put some fresh ideas on the table.

Look at problems as opportunities for growth and change, and you won't be troubled by them—just challenged to greater accomplishments.

Problem solving is always the right solution.

Slow down and live a little.

If a man does not keep pace with his companions, perhaps it is because he hears a different drummer. Let him step to the music which he hears, however measured or far away.

—Henry David Thoreau

PACE

The next time you make your commute, listen to the traffic report on the radio. Count the number of traffic accidents that occur during the hour or two when people are doing nothing else but driving to work. Many people would live longer—literally—if they would simply slow down.

That's true on the highway and in other aspects of life.

We live in an over stressed world, and it's killing us. Stress is one of the primary reasons people visit a doctor, and it's linked with nearly every ailment from stomach ulcers to heart disease. Stress causes problems in family life as well.

Slow your life down and enjoy it once in a while.

When you have vacation and personal days off from work, use them.

Take a look at your calendar and ask, "Which of these activities are really essential?" Unplug, sit back, and relax. You won't believe how much fun it is to be alive.

Slow down before you come to a complete stop.

Love your kids.

Children have more need
of models than critics.

—Joseph Joubert

CHILDREN

If you're a parent, God has given you one of the greatest privileges on earth. He's entrusted you with the care of His children—your children.

Unfortunately, you may be so busy providing for your kids that you overlook the thing they need most—you! The years when your kids are at home are the years you're busy establishing a career, working hard, and moving up. All those activities are important, but remember that these precious gifts will live under your roof for less than twenty years. Now is the time to pour your love into them.

Discipline your children so they know how to live.

Love your children so they have a sense of security.

Teach your children so they gain self-confidence.

Praise your children so they gain self-esteem.

Give yourself to your kids, just as you'd like a loving father to do for you. That's the way God planned it. He modeled parenting, and He gave you a Manual of Operations: the Bible.

Kids need more than food to grow; they need love.

Recognize the greatest miracle of life.

Hope is the companion of
power, and mother of success,
for who so hopes strongly has
within him the gift of miracles.

—Samuel Smiles

MIRACLES

It happens every day, though you may never notice. All around you, miracles are taking place. Flowers bloom. Trees bud. Little birds take flight. Children are born. The miracle of life is renewed millions of times every twenty-four hours. Do you ever stop to notice?

Here's the greatest miracle of all—your life. You are alive, enjoying the gift of creation that God has given to us. Celebrate the gift of life.

Stop for a minute today and think about the fact that you're alive. Thank God for the miracle of life.

Look out the window and count the number of living things you see. Remember that God made each one.

When you tuck you kids in tonight, marvel at the miracle that they were born from your flesh, living reminders of God's precious gift.

Thank the Creator for friends and family.

God has done a great thing in the world. He has given you life. Praise Him.

Grade God's miracles with a "See."

Avoid
road rage.

Remember that happiness
is a way of travel,
not a destination.

—Roy Goodman

TRAVEL

A tenth of a second. That's about how much time it takes to travel sixteen feet—the length of a car—on a freeway. So the next time someone cuts in front of you during rush hour, ask yourself, "Is it worth getting angry over a tenth of a second?"

Road rage makes headlines when commuter disputes erupt into violence, but all of us are prone to become angry when treated badly on the highway. Careless drivers are rude, at the very least, and downright dangerous at the worst. While traveling at high speeds in tight traffic, it's easy for tempers to flare. You say things you regret. You're tempted to drive aggressively. Maybe you return the favor to someone else by cutting off another driver.

Don't do it. Don't let the person who cut you off in traffic wreck your day. Life is way too short.

Gain control of your emotions behind the wheel. Remember that there is no insult worth risking your life—or anyone else's. Be cool behind the wheel.

Take the high road on the highway.

Put a little love in your life.

When love and skill work
together expect a masterpiece.

—John Ruskin

LOVE

The stereotype is that women are more romantic than men are. It's not true. Both men and women are romantic, but we tend to express it in different ways. So go ahead, start expressing.

Put a little love into your life by giving your wife some romance on her terms. Here are some ideas:

Purchase some flowers on your way home from work—just because.

Take her out to eat on a Tuesday.

Book a room at one of those bed-and-breakfast places and take her away for the weekend.

Put some chocolate into her lunch bag.

Send her a romantic e-mail.

Do the dishes every night for a week.

Put the kids to bed.

Pay her a sincere compliment.

Tell her how much you love her—out loud.

Look for little ways to light up the life of your lover. Think about her needs and put her first. She'll do the same for you.

Love is like a four-way stop: Right always goes first.

Spend time with good friends.

Without friends no one would choose to live, though he had all other goods.

—Aristotle

FRIENDSHIP

You can't do life alone, and you don't have to. Life is meant to be a partnership, lived in community with family and friends.

Other than your spouse or close family members, whom do you count as friends? Develop friendships and maintain them by spending time together. You may have to take the initiative. But go ahead. Making friends is one of the most important things to do. You need to interact with others—to expand your interests, to learn. And friendship is a good starting point.

Take an afternoon off and play golf with a couple of buddies.

Go to dinner with your wife and another couple.

Get involved in a small group at your church.

And don't forget that the way to have a friend is to be one. Lend a hand to a neighbor who is working in the yard. Give a word of encouragement to a new family at church. Always offer a smile and some positive words.

Friends are for *life*.

Have a special cause.

Compassion is the basis
of all morality.

—Arthur Schopenhauer

COMPASSION

It's possible that your vocation will not be the work that brings fulfillment to your life. You may be a construction foreman, yet long to do more than erect buildings. You may be an accountant, yet have an inner passion to see lives changed. You may be an engineer, yet have a desire to bring healing to the broken.

Act on that desire to do good by investing your time and energy in a compassionate cause.

There are needs all around you. Even the most ideal community will have residents who suffer from hunger, abuse, drug addiction, or homelessness. Read the newspaper or talk with area pastors to find out what's happening around you. Then get involved.

Volunteer your time.

Share your skills.

Become a mentor.

You can't change the whole world, but you can change the lives of those near you. Your life can be more than a career. It can be a compassionate cause. Your talent, your time, and your resources are just what are needed.

Give until it feels good.

Give someone a hug.

Talk not of wasted affection,

affection never was wasted.

—Henry Wadsworth Longfellow

AFFECTION

Did you ever notice that dogs and cats thrive on affection. They'll sidle up to you, nuzzle your hand, and practically beg for a pat on the head, no matter what has happened that day.

People are not much different. We all need affection.

You can brighten the day of just about anyone with the expression of appropriate affection. When a coworker receives some bad news, a hand on the shoulder and a kind word may mean more than a pay increase. Affection is a way to say, "I care about what has happened to you."

When your children have a reason to celebrate, give them a bear hug! Affection is a way to say, "I care about what you have done."

Be quick to offer a kind touch, a hand on the arm, a warm handshake, and a listening ear. Let someone know you care. You can break down the affection barrier in a safe and wholesome way.

Besides, people are more important than puppies.

Shut your mouth when angry.

A fool gives full vent to his anger, but a wise man keeps himself under control.

—Proverbs 29:11

EMOTIONS

Knowing the right thing to say is about half of what it takes to be considered a wise person. Knowing when to say nothing at all is the other half.

Keeping your mouth shut is a sure way to be viewed as wise, especially when emotions run high. Usually when we get angry, our first response is to pop off with a quick retort or a jibe. Doing so may vent some personal anger, but it usually damages relationships, hurts your reputation, and generally makes the situation worse.

Learn how to control your temper by learning to control your tongue. Count to ten before speaking. Leave the room. Change the subject. Or make a "creative exit." Do anything rather than letting your words be spilled in anger. Such a mess is tough to clean up.

Remember, God is patient with you. He accepts you as you are and has made it possible for you to be even better than you are.

Watch your heart, and prevent thorns from growing up into your words.

Strive for excellence.

I am careful not to confuse excellence with perfection. Excellence, I can reach for, perfection is God's business.

—Michael J. Fox

EXCELLENCE

Excellence is a quality that everyone respects. We associate it with fine automobiles, expensive clothes, and premier restaurants. Not everyone can afford quality, but everybody wants it. And everyone should strive for it.

Here's the good news. You *can* have quality in your personal life. You can choose to be a person of excellence.

Decide that you will do your very best on the job, regardless of whether or not the boss notices.

Resolve to be a person of integrity, always telling the truth, never breaking your word.

Keep your home and possessions in top shape. You may not have an expensive car, but you can keep the one you have looking like a million bucks!

Present yourself well, and keep your appearance up. You don't have to have the latest fashions, but you'll do well to have the neatest and cleanest.

Strive for excellence in everything that you do. You can afford it. It only takes practice, pressing, and persistence.

Make sure the "e" in your l-i-f-e stands for "excellence."

Stop and smell the coffee.

If a man insisted always on
being serious, and never
allowed himself to relax,
he would go much
or become unstable
without ever knowing it.

—Herodotus

RELAXATION

What's on your list for Saturday? Mow the lawn? Clean out the garage? Run some errands? Go to your daughter's basketball game? Weekends can be just as busy as workdays—sometimes more so.

Don't forget to do something important for yourself this weekend—nothing.

Take some time to relax and simply enjoy doing nothing. Give yourself permission to take an hour or two off. Put on a fresh pot of coffee, browse the newspaper, and simply enjoy yourself. Dust off the patio furniture and prepare yourself for a serious break.

You don't have to let your responsibilities slide. The danger is that you'll do just the opposite, that you'll become a slave to your schedule. Take control of your life by letting it go. Take some time just for yourself, and relax.

Work is what you do to help you make a living. But living is what you do to help your work. So live a little. Trade the business suit for some "scuffies."

Take a break so you won't break.

Quit something.

A man too busy to take
care of his health is like
a mechanic too busy to
take care of his tools.

—A Spanish Proverb

BUSYNESS

Take out your planner and review your schedule for the month. How many things do you have scheduled outside of work and worship? You may have a sports league one night a week, a civic club one Saturday a month, and a few committee meetings scattered around. And that's before you add in kids' schedules, school sports, and your wife's activities.

Don't you ever get tired?

If you're constantly saying to yourself "I'm way too busy," then you are. Take the cue from your subconscious and quit something. Yes, quit something.

That doesn't make you a quitter. It puts you in control of your life—rather than being out of control.

Take a hard look at your goals for your personal life, your spiritual life, and your family life. Then see which of your extra-curricular activities contribute to reaching your goals, and which are simply dead weight.

Like a circus lion tamer, grab a whip and a chair, and tame that schedule. Put that planner in its corner, and then take a bow to life.

Develop the mind
of a learner.

A good education should
leave much to be desired.

—Alan Gregg

EDUCATION

When was the last time you learned something? I suppose we all learn something every day by experience. But when was the last time you set out to inquire about something in the world that you did not understand?

Cultivate the habit of learning. Become a person who is curious about the surrounding environment. Then satisfy that curiosity by learning new things.

Pick up a book about the Vietnam War and learn something new.

Tour a manufacturing plant and find out something about how autos are made.

Get a telescope and take a look at the stars.

It's a big world out there. Even if you attended college or graduate school, you didn't scratch the surface of all the information that's packed into God's great world. Don't allow your mind to stick in neutral. Become a lifelong learner. Strive to know more tomorrow than you do today.

Your mind is one of the few things you can expand without breaking it.

Learn the value of sweat equity.

All work is seed down.
It grows and spreads,
and sows itself anew.

—Thomas Carlyle

WORK

Contrary to popular belief, *work* is not a four-letter word. Working hard gives you a feeling of accomplishment, and it adds value to your life. Work is a way to add strength to the skill that God has given to you. So when you work, you worship.

Don't allow people to outwork you on the job. Others may be stronger, younger, or smarter, but if you work as diligently as you can, your light will shine just as brightly.

Learn to enjoy the work you do at home. Don't allow your household chores to become drudgery. Take pride in the work you do in maintaining your automobile and other possessions. Everything you have is a sacred trust from God. Be a good steward of what He has entrusted to you.

Teach your kids to work. Let them see that accomplishing something can be fun, and give them a reward for doing it. You can add value to anything you choose, if you'll work with a purpose in view.

Hard work may not keep you off the unemployment line, but it will keep you on the *enjoyment* line.

Study life from the perspective of tennis.

If life doesn't offer a
game worth playing,
then invent a new one.

—Anthony J. D'Angelo

GAME

Tennis is an interesting game, and it's a lot like life. For one thing, it's played on a court according to strict rules. So is your life. Live within the bounds of a society and abide by its laws.

Tennis always begins with a serve; and so does each day. Every morning, you begin with a fresh possibility. Make the most of it.

Like life, tennis is a game of volleys. You won't win them all, but you won't lose them all either. If you learn to recover, charge the net once in a while, and develop a strong backhand, you'll get through it okay.

Tennis is a game of endurance, and so is your life. A tennis match can go on for hours, and often becomes more a test of stamina than of skill. Determination is your greatest ally off the court as well. If you make up your mind to persevere, you can achieve nearly anything.

Someone once said, "I don't play tennis because I don't want to be involved in a game where love means nothing." Make love your motivation for every goal you strive to accomplish—love for God and for other people.

Life isn't just about tennis and points, it's about good plays along the way.

Seek to become more hospitable.

Treat others as you
want to be treated.

—The Golden Rule

HOSPITALITY

In the ancient world, hospitality was one of the greatest virtues. In the days before Hampton Inns and Comfort Suites dotted the landscape, weary travelers depended on the hospitality of strangers for their comfort and security. These days, hospitality is a lost art.

Revive it.

When your church hosts missionaries or other guests, open your home to them. You'll provide a valued service, and you'll have the joy of making new friends.

When there are newcomers to your church or workplace, host a gathering in your home, inviting some newcomers and some established team members. Over a casual meal or a cup of coffee, relationships blossom.

In the course of an ordinary day, look for ways to play the host to your coworkers and friends. Hold the door for someone. Offer to bring coffee to others at a meeting. Share your bag of candy with a cubicle mate.

Those small acts of hospitality say "I value you." They set a tone for teamwork and togetherness that will make everyone's day brighter.

Don't be too competitive.

The ability to focus attention on important things is a defining characteristic of intelligence.

—Robert J. Shiller

COMPETITION

Men love to compete. It's part of our nature. We compete in sports, business, and even conversation. There's just something about the way God made us; we all want to be number one.

For the most part, competition is healthy and spurs us on to achievement. Part of the reason we are successful in our careers is that we have a natural drive to excel.

But competition can be unhealthy too. Our drive to achieve can lead us to do things that we regret. Friendly softball games can get out of hand when the will to win is supreme. Competition in business can take a nasty turn when it drives competitors to be deceptive or break the law.

When you try to better yourself at the expense of another, both parties end up hurt.

Temper your will to win with a desire to maintain integrity and good relationships. Never let your drive to excel cloud your view of what matters most: your relationship with God and with others.

You don't have to compete for God's attention. You already have it.

Say no to temptation.

Temptation rarely comes in
working hours. It is in their
leisure time that men
are made or marred.

—W. M. Taylor

CHOICES

It's there all the time, like a nagging ache or a low burn. Usually, it's not hard to control, but it's always there. Temptation.

Everyone faces temptation, and most of us have a particular area of vulnerability. For most men, that area is sex. Some guys are tempted to adultery or pornography. Others simply deal with lustful thoughts.

For other men, money is the temptation. They covet possessions and are tempted to lie, cheat, or steal in order to obtain them.

Anger, alcohol, drugs—there's a long list of things that can tempt a man, but there's a single answer to all of them: faith.

Determine to live your life God's way, and stand on that choice when you face temptation. Make up your mind now that you will be a man of character, and then begin to make the choices that will take you out of harm's way.

You make dozens of choices every day. Choose the one that has an everlasting effect: Say no to temptation.

Knock long at the door of opportunity.

Never let your persistence
and passion turn into
stubbornness and ignorance.

—Anthony J. D'Angelo

PERSISTENCE

Everyone knows that Thomas Edison invented the light bulb. But most people don't know that he tried more than one thousand experiments before he perfected this miracle of modern lighting. He tried a thousand times, and he failed.

I'm glad he tried experiment number 1,001.

You may not succeed on your first try—or your second, or your third. But you will succeed if you continue to learn and refuse to give up.

You may not make it into college on your first try, but keep going. Take another entrance exam. Make another trip to the financial aid office. You can do it! You can get that degree.

You probably won't get the first job you apply for, but that's okay. Some employer will recognize the skills you have to offer.

Your first business idea may not be a winner, but you are. Keep working, and you'll make it.

There are very few geniuses in the world. Most people succeed on pure perseverance. And you have plenty of that.

Discipline your thought life.

Self discipline is that which
next to virtue, truly and
essentially raises one
man above another.

—Joseph Addison

DISCIPLINE

Would you invite into your home a guest who insulted your wife, told lewd jokes, needled you into skipping work, and wasted your money? Hardly.

Then why would you invite that same person into your mind?

Take a mental inventory of your thought life for the past twenty-four hours. If you're like many men, your thought patterns will be revealing. There might be some inappropriate thoughts, some not-so-nice remarks, a little bit of dangerous daydreaming, and some wasted work time.

Don't do things in your mind that you would never do in real life. Discipline your thought life.

Reject inappropriate sexual thoughts. Don't let them stay long enough to get comfortable.

Refuse to be rude or demeaning to others, even in your imagination.

Don't fantasize about living a lifestyle that you know is not really for you.

It's been said that integrity is what you are like when no one is around. That saying is never more true than in the most private of all places—your own mind.

Open your heart to God.

If we confess our sins, he is faithful and just and will forgive us our sins and purify us from all unrighteousness.

—1 John 1:9

SALVATION

You've probably made up your mind about many things in life—education, career, marriage. Maybe you've chosen a favorite football team or a favorite NASCAR driver.

But there's one thing you need to keep an open mind about—your relationship with Jesus Christ. If you've never made up your mind about this all-important aspect of your life, here's how you can. It's as simple as ABC:

A—Admit that you are a sinner (Romans 3:23). *For all have sinned and fall short of the glory of God.*

B—Believe that God sent Jesus to pay the punishment for your sin (John 1:12). *Yet to all who received him, to those who believed in his name, he gave the right to become children of God.*

C—Confess that you are sorry for sin and declare that Jesus Christ is now number one in your life (Romans 10:9-10). *If you confess with your mouth, "Jesus is Lord," and believe in your heart that God raised him from the dead, you will be saved. For it is with your heart that you believe and are justified, and it is with your mouth that you confess and are saved.*

Here's a prayer you might want to pray:

"Lord Jesus, I admit that I have sinned against You. I am sorry for my sin, and I trust You to forgive me. I invite You to come into my life and help me to live for You all the days of my life. Amen."

Make a list of goals and dreams.

We go where our vision is.

—Joseph Murphy

VISION

Where do you want to be this time next year? In five years? When will your house be paid for? What do you hope to accomplish by age forty?

Draw a roadmap for your life by making a list of goals and dreams. Share them with a trusted friend or mentor. Committing these targets to paper will make them easier to hit.

Write a five- and ten-year plan for your career. You can change your objectives later, but it will help to have some idea of where you hope to be.

Make a one-year, three-year, and five-year plan for your finances. Then make a long-term plan that includes your retirement. Even if you're under thirty, it's not too early to make this plan.

List the things you hope to accomplish in your personal and spiritual life. Target your educational aims or other self-improvement goals. Writing your goals will help bring them to life.

If you don't plan it, you probably won't do it.

Use your talents at church.

Act as if what you do makes
a difference. It does!

—William James

INVOLVEMENT

Okay, so your career is going well. You've started a family. You've made the down payment on a house, and you've sold the van and bought an SUV. You have a lot going for yourself.

What are you doing for others?

If everything in life centers on you (or your family), then you're missing something important. Real fulfillment comes not from what you gain for yourself but from what you give to others.

Your church is the perfect place to begin. You can use your talents and abilities there to enhance the lives of others.

Volunteer to sing on the praise team or serve as an usher.

Ask the youth director if he or she could use an extra volunteer.

Consider using your professional skill as an accountant, lawyer, or doctor in one of the ministries of your congregation. You have a lot to offer, and your talents will do much good. Put them to work at church.

You haven't begun to give until you've put yourself in the offering plate.

Be "high touch" as well as high tech.

What we do with
technology will determine
its benefit or harm.

—Newton Minow

TECHNOLOGY

Technology has revolutionized our world almost overnight. Fewer than twenty years ago, *Time* magazine declared the personal computer "man of the year." In that short span of time, the microchip has taken over everything from our work (Can you imagine an office without a computer?) to conversations (Could you survive without a cell phone?) to our homes (DVD, anyone?).

Most of the changes have been for the better, but some are for the worse. While we travel, work, and communicate with less effort, we face new dangers as well. Stalkers use the Internet to prey upon children; pornographers shove their filthy wares at use through unwanted e-mail; and cell phone calls can interrupt our thoughts anytime, anywhere.

Make the most of the technology available, but don't let it get the best of you. Make a covenant with your eyes; agree that you will not look at improper material. Limit the intrusion of technology into your home; set a limit on the number of hours you watch television or electronic entertainment each week. Don't allow technology to replace personal human contact in your family life. Schedule times when you shut off the video games, turn off the cell phones, and have a good, old-fashioned conversation.

Remember, you control the "Off" button.

Release
the past.

Forgiveness means
letting go of the past.

—Gerald Jampolsky

FORGIVENESS

It still hurts, doesn't it? You can still hear the words she said when she broke up with you. Perhaps the speech from the executive director still rings in your ears. The word *downsizing* took on a whole new meaning when it was applied to you. It might have been a neighbor, an old girlfriend, a family member, or even a complete stranger, but everyone has been hurt by someone.

Here's something you may not know. Nursing the grudge only makes it hurt worse. Remembering an old wound is like rubbing salt into it; it just stings all the more. The only way to get rid of the past is to forgive. The words of Jesus on the cross, "Father forgive," remind us of the importance of loving people regardless of what they've done to us.

It sounds impossible, doesn't it? Letting go of the anger from a past hurt is not easy. It means surrendering your right to hurt someone else in the way that they hurt you. No, it isn't easy, but it is the only path to freedom.

Forgive. Then you can finally get past your past.

Be generous
to a fault.

The habit of giving only

enhances the desire to give.

—Walt Whitman

BENEVOLENCE

What you keep, you never use. What you give away, you get back time and again. That's another way of saying something that Jesus once said: "Give, and it will be given to you" (Luke 6:38). It's the law of generosity. When you are generous with others, they are generous with you.

Our temptation is to hold on to our possessions and money so tightly that our knuckles turn white. What's mine is mine. I worked for it, and I deserve to keep every penny.

Those who practice generosity have discovered a different principle at work. They know that giving to others is the best way to receive. We are blessed in order to bless others.

When you give generous gifts, you build up a bank of good will.

When you give to someone in need, you help a neighbor and, therefore, help yourself.

When you give the gift of your time, you build relationships with friends.

When you give love to someone who is hurting, you bring healing.

Don't be a miser with your time, talent, and treasure. Give yourself away. That's the secret to true riches.

Giving is living.

Allow your ideas to percolate.

There are only two kinds of scholars; those who love ideas and those who hate them.

—Emile Chartier

IDEAS

Chances are you probably have some money stashed away in a retirement account. And if you're wise, you're adding to it on a regular basis. You don't intend to use the money right now; you are giving it time to grow. Later on, the relatively few dollars that you've invested will pay handsome dividends.

Ideas are much that way. You have to invest them, stash them away, and give them time to grow.

Start an idea bank and put a good thought into it once in a while. If you're in a creative business, jot down new product ideas and put them in a file.

If others work for you, hand out a steady stream of ideas for free at your staff meeting. Then stand back and see if any of them take root.

When you observe someone else doing their job well, take good mental notes and remember how the work was done. Tuck the idea in your mind and see if it develops some application for your own work.

A mind without ideas is a desert. Plant some good ideas in your mind, and observe how they grow.

Live justly.

Half-right is not right at all.

—J. B. Gambrell

JUSTICE

"There is no justice, in or out of court." That statement, famously attributed to the legendary American jurist Clarence Darrow, can seem quite true at times. We often hear news stories about innocent people who are unfairly punished and criminals who are released without consequence. Financial scandals, insider trading, bribes, corruption—where is the justice?

It's tempting to think that because the world seems unfair, our own actions have no consequence. But they do. We have limited control over the justice system, but we can control our own actions and help ensure justice for those with whom we come in contact.

Start with yourself. Follow the rules at home, on the road, and at work. Tell the truth on your tax return. Be fair with your children.

Then widen the circle, working to ensure justice for those around you. See to it that your kids treat each other fairly. Stick up for your employees. Take notice of what's happening in your community. When others are treated unfairly, speak up for them.

Take care to remember, though, that justice is ultimately in the hands of our all-knowing God. When dealing with others, always err on the side of mercy, just as our loving Father does for us.

Be just in your actions and merciful in your judgments.

You can make justice a reality in your world.

Get up and get going.

Ability is what you're capable of doing. Motivation determines what you do. Attitude determines how well you do it.

—Lon Holtz

MOTIVATION

Getting started is the hardest part of any task. Once you begin, the work seems to move along. But starting into motion—that's the tough part.

Here are some good ideas for getting yourself primed for action.

Become a morning person. The first three hours of your day are the most productive. You'll get more done at the office between 7:00 and 10:00 A.M. than in the rest of the day combined. Get up and get started.

Avoid distractions. Don't steal a glance at the classified ads or go back for that second cup of coffee and stand and chat with anyone who walks by. Settle down and get to work.

Develop a start-up routine. Football players stretch. Baseball players take batting practice. Find the five- or ten-minute routine that will say to your mind and body "It's time to work."

Work from a plan. Unstructured time is the least productive. Every day, make a list of the things you need to do, and then rank them in order of priority.

Do the first thing first, and you'll last.

Don't speak too soon.

The first step to getting
the things you want
out of life is this:
Decide what you want.

—Ben Stein

DECISIVENESS

According to the old saying, it's better to keep your mouth shut and be thought a fool than to open it and remove all doubt. Look around you. You've probably spotted a few folks who should have chosen silence over speaking.

Avoid quick judgments, and avoid quick statements even more. Develop a reputation as a cool-headed thinker, someone whose judgment can be trusted. Use your head before you use your mouth. When you finally speak, what you say will make more sense and usually be less destructive.

The Bible compares the tongue to a rudder. (See James 3:4-5.) If you've ever done any sailing, you know how important it is to keep the rudder under control.

Being slow to speak is not the same as being indecisive. Examine the evidence, make up your mind, and state your decision. Sometimes you'll have to do so quickly. But usually, there will be time to weigh your options and make a sound determination.

Volume doesn't always add quality. Use sound judgment.

Live the truth instead of professing it.

Integrity combined with
faithfulness is a powerful force
and worthy of great respect.

—Unknown

INTEGRITY

Many people proclaim their views loudly, nearly making pests of themselves by commenting on the moral decline of our culture. Unfortunately, some of those same people fail to live up to the high standard they profess.

Make it your habit to act first and speak later. Seek to become known for your integrity, not as someone who simply *talks* about integrity.

When other people can say of you "He's honest, fair, and upright," then you'll have the moral authority to talk about those virtues with others.

Actions speak louder than words. Remember that your actions are talking a mile-a-minute, even when you're not saying a thing. In life, a "walker" is better than a "talker." Preaching without practice usually means a short career in the "pulpit."

Remember that God is the source of integrity. His Word, the Bible, is a daily guidebook for living a moral life in a relative age.

It's not who you say you are that matters; it's who you are.

Sow kindness into the lives of people.

The best portions of a good man's life—his little, nameless, unremembered acts of kindness and love.

—William Wordsworth

KINDNESS

We live in a cruel world. That sounds like a cliché, but it's often quite true. Every day, someone around you is facing adversity and could use some understanding.

A coworker gets laid off.

The wife of a friend is diagnosed with cancer.

Your neighbor has a traffic accident. He's okay, but his car will never recover.

These are opportunities to sow some kindness into the hard ground of life. You can make life easier for the people you know through consideration and generosity.

Say hello to the people you pass at work, even if you can't remember their names.

Offer a helping hand when someone is in obvious need.

Let others take the best parking spots.

Let it slide when a harried partner at work makes a typing mistake on her report.

Yield right of way to that impatient driver.

Do to other people exactly what you like for them to do for you. If everybody did that, what a great world it would be!

Kindness sees a need and fills it.

Confront your impossibilities.

Dedication is not what others
expect of you, it is what
you can give to others.

—Unknown

DEDICATION

They're out there—waiting for you, looming in the distance. They're the impossible barriers, the ones you know you can't climb.

You want to get the project done this year, but the weeks are slipping by too fast.

You want to finish that degree, but your wife is expecting another child.

You dream of that trip around the world, but your health isn't what it used to be.

What will you do about the impossible dreams in your life? Ignore them? Cling to them? Leave them alone?

Why not find a way to make them possible?

Very few things are truly impossible. Most of the things we think are impossible simply require more dedication and ingenuity than we first thought.

When you reach one of those impossible barriers, back up, size it up, and find a way to get around. Cultivate your skills. Employ the talents of others. Read. Learn. Copy the best of the best around you. You can succeed.

Barriers aren't as tall as your dogged dedication.

Measure wealth by what's not for sale.

The secret of a good life
is to have the right loyalties
and hold them in the
right scale of values.

—Norman Thomas

VALUES

Most people measure their wealth by what they own. You've probably played that game. You drive through traffic and notice the cars that are nicer than yours. Your car has become your status symbol. You see a "For Sale" sign on a nice home and wonder if it's time to move up. The home that you own says something about you.

The dragon of materialism has crept into our society. Trying to stay even with others is a game that can be depressing because it's a game you can never win. There's always someone who has more than you!

Here's another way to measure your wealth. Judge your worth by what's not for sale in your life.

Your house may be on the market, but your integrity isn't.

You may consider trading in your old car, but you've determined to be faithful to your family.

The interest rate on your mortgage may be negotiable, but your honesty is a non-negotiable.

A job promotion may have a price tag, but you're not in the market.

You have character, pride, and integrity. Man, you're rich!

Make the most of every day.

Decide what you want,
decide what you are willing to
exchange for it. Establish your
priorities and go to work.

—H. L. Hunt

PRIORITIES

If you were given $1,440 every day, what would you spend it on? You might travel, buy something for the house, or go out to eat. But I'm sure of what you wouldn't do. You wouldn't spend $240 to rent a television set for one day, and I'm sure you wouldn't spend $60 on a telephone call.

Yet many people do.

You see, we do get 1,440 every day—minutes, that is. And some of us spend four hours or more watching television or an hour in idle chitchat. We spend the opportunity of a lifetime. We cash out the one account that will give us one of the greater returns.

Make the most of your time (and your money too) by setting priorities. Spend some time on leisure, but not the whole amount. Spend some time on planning, but be sure to work your plan. Spend some time on others, but be sure to leave some time for yourself.

If you've "got a minute," you have a lot!

Guard your reputation.

You can't build a reputation
on what you are going to do.

—Henry Ford

REPUTATION

Your reputation is like a set of antique golf clubs. It's one of a kind, priceless, and irreplaceable. If you break it, there's no way to replace it.

Guard your reputation as you guard your life. Don't sacrifice it for a few dollars or a few moments of pleasure. Don't allow even the hint of scandal to taint your good name.

Keep your word. Always do what you've said you will do. If you make a promise, then keep it. If you say you will, do it.

Handle money with scrupulous honesty. Never allow a question to arise about your financial integrity. Don't cheat God. Don't cheat Uncle Sam.

Pay your bills on time; keep your credit clear. Your money trail will always be hot. And somebody is always on it.

Treat women with modesty and respect. Be faithful to your wife and children. Someone not only needs you but also wants to be just like you.

You can buy fame, but you can't buy a good name.

Take "what if" out of your vocabulary.

Few things in the world are more powerful than a positive push. A smile, a word of optimism and hope.

—Richard M. DeVos

OPTIMISM

Don't sing the "what if" blues. If you do, you'll always be out of tune. Life is linear, not circular. You can't go back, so you might as well go on. You can be positive, even about the negative circumstances in your life.

Take the "what if" words completely out of your vocabulary. Here's how.

First, quit looking back at the past. Don't allow yourself to wonder, "What if I'd gone to college?" or "What if I'd taken another career path?" The past is gone. Let it go. Look through the windshield, not the rearview mirror.

Second, quit asking "what if" about the future. Don't wonder, "What if I changed jobs?" If you want to make the change, do it! Don't ask yourself, "What if we moved?" If it fits with your long-term goals, do it!

The world lies before you. You can accomplish great things in life. But you will never accomplish them by wondering. Great things are achieved only by doing.

Give work your best effort.

We work to become,

not to acquire.

—Elbert Hubbard

LABOR

You get what you give in life, and that's especially true of your workplace. What you get out of your work—in every way—depends largely on what you put into it. Your work performance will not only make a difference to your boss; it will ultimately make a difference to you.

Do your best at work, and you will be rewarded. People will notice that you work hard. You may get a pay raise, or you may not. Either way, you'll become a leader in your workplace. And leaders are rewarded over time.

Do your best at work, and you will be respected. Your supervisor may not know who the best producers are, but everyone else does. When you give your best effort, you'll gain the respect of your peers.

Do your best at work, and you will love what you do. Aim to reach high every day, and you'll feel better about what you are doing.

Become a better laborer, and you'll become a better producer.

Be gentle with your spouse.

He who finds a wife
finds what is good.

—Proverbs 18:22

MARRIAGE

You're probably bigger than your wife, taller perhaps, and certainly stronger. That's true physically, and it may be true in some other ways as well. Generally, men and women have a different emotional makeup. We like to bear down on a problem and "just do it." They're usually more concerned about feelings, relationships—the softer side of things.

That difference means you may need to be careful in communicating with your wife. Be aware of her feelings and vulnerabilities, and do what you can to meet her needs—emotionally and spiritually, as well as physically.

Speak gently, even when you are upset. Strong words have great power to harm. Softer words have a healing power.

Be considerate of her need to talk. She may need to discuss things that seem minute to you, but they are important to her. Women may not be the weaker sex, but they are often the gentler one.

Be gentle with your wife. After all, she is a gift from God.

Learn to listen.

No man ever listened

himself out of a job!

—Calvin Coolidge

ATTENTIVENESS

"**Y**eah."

"In a minute."

"Not now. "

"Wait a sec—."

We rattle them off without thinking; those pat phrases that communicate a very obvious message: I'm busy; leave me alone.

Our world is already moving too quickly for comfort. We make it worse when we fail to slow down and listen to those around us.

Develop the habits of a good listener.

Look up when you're speaking to someone. Don't bury your face in the newspaper or the computer screen.

Make eye contact during conversation. Doing so lets others know that you're tuned in to what they're saying.

Listen without interrupting. Let the other person finish before offering an answer or an assessment.

Communication is even more important today than it used to be, and much more complicated—instant messages, text messaging, e-mail. We have the latest technology, but it's often easier to use these devices in place of face-to-face encounters. The personal touch is still more important.

Paying attention communicates respect.

Reflect on past successes and failures.

The real man smiles in trouble,
gathers strength from distress,
and grows brave by reflection.

—Thomas Paine

LANDMARKS

What have you learned over the past twenty or thirty years? If the answer is "Nothing," you have a problem.

Your life has been a laboratory for success and failure, and you've probably had your share of both. The great thing about failure is the worst thing about success—it's never permanent. Whether you've just won or lost, you start a new game every day.

Learn what you can from the trips and triumphs of the past.

When you were successful, look for the factors that took your there. What things did you do right? What pitfalls did you avoid? Who helped you along the way? Did you just get lucky?

When you failed, find out why. Where were the errors in judgment? What did you simply fail to do? Who provided the greatest resistance? Could you do better next time?

Ready or not, the sun comes up every morning. You can prepare yourself for a new day by taking some time to reflect on the one that's just passed.

Cultivate your devotional life.

Prayer does not change God,
but changes him who prays.

—Søren Kierkegeard

PRAYER

What do you pay per month for your cellular phone service? And how many "free" minutes do you get for that fee? Even if your call time is unlimited, you're still paying something for the privilege of using the network.

Here's a better deal. Get connected to God through prayer. There is no installation charge, no monthly fee, and all the minutes really are free.

Cultivate your devotional life by talking with God every day. Carve out some time in your busy schedule to make an appointment. Put it in your planner, and then do it.

Make this conversation a two-way communication. Tell God what's on your mind. Let Him know what frightens or frustrates you. Ask for His help with the problems you face.

Then listen to what He has to say. Shhh. Just be quiet for a few minutes. You'll hear His voice, speaking loud and clear.

Read the Bible. He has already expressed His feelings about you.

There are no "roaming charges" with God. You'll always be in His coverage area.

Say thank you often.

Gratitude is born in hearts
that take time to
count up past mercies.

—Charles E. Jefferson

GRATITUDE

I've heard it said that dogs are the only animals on earth that will work for praise alone. It's not true. Human beings will do nearly anything just to hear those two simple words: "Thank you."

The best part of saying thanks is that it's completely free. It costs you nothing to show your gratitude to others, and it gives them one of the most valuable rewards—encouragement.

Say thank you to your wife and kids, just for being part of your family.

Let your friend know how much you appreciated that birthday gift.

Say thanks to the store clerk who hands you your change, and smile.

Express your appreciation to your pastor, your boss, and your employees. Let them know that you appreciate the role they play in your life.

Say thanks to anybody who does a job well, whether they did the job for you or not.

A good "thank you" is worth a million dollars—and you can hand thanks out like peanuts!

Go out on a limb with God.

I show you doubt, to prove that faith exists.

—Robert Browning

FAITH

If you're waiting for proof, there isn't any. In spite of all the books that promise irrefutable evidence that God is real and that He loves you, these are truths you simply have to take on faith.

It takes faith to believe that God is real. You can't see Him. But you can know Him. Believe it.

It takes faith to believe that God loves you. Bad things happen in life. But God is still good. Trust Him.

It takes faith to believe in an eternal home called heaven, a place where there is no sorrow and where you can live forever. But that place does exist. Know it.

It takes faith to accept Jesus Christ as God's Son and to trust your entire life to Him. But He is trustworthy. Follow Him.

You may say that you just can't believe. If that's true, you'd never put the key in your car ignition. You'd never sit on a folding chair. Belief is all around you, and you practice it every day.

Go ahead. Take the leap of faith.

Finish well.

Great works are performed

not by strength,

but by perseverance.

—Samuel Johnson

PERSEVERANCE

Hundreds of people have set out to climb Mt. Everest. Only a handful of them have made it to the top. It isn't starting something that gets you into the history books. It's finishing.

You've started well in life in many ways.

You've started your education, perhaps, or you have started a career. Maybe you have married and started a family. You've begun the journey of faith by accepting Jesus Christ. You've started well.

Now you must finish well.

Don't be distracted by lesser pursuits. Finish the education that you began.

Don't be derailed by dishonesty. Finish strong in your career.

Don't be diverted by temptation. Finish your marriage with the faithfulness that you pledged in the beginning.

Don't become discouraged by doubts. Keep strong in the faith, and finish the race you started.

You'll pass them along the way—the faint of heart, the weary, the fair-weather travelers. But you keep your eyes on the prize, and keep going.

Finish strong in the race of life.

Stay humble.

Life is a long lesson in humility.

—James M. Barrie

PRIDE

Someone once said that if you toot your own horn, you'll usually get the pitch too high. True humility is a mark of character; false pride is a blemish. An exaggerated opinion of yourself is not only misleading to others; it keeps you from reaching your full potential.

Of course, not all pride is bad. A certain amount is necessary to succeed. But false pride is damaging. It makes unreasonable demands on you. It causes others to lose respect for you.

Work on your humility. Come to terms with the fact that your skills are God given. You can only do what He equips you to do.

Don't put yourself on a pedestal. Appreciate the worth of others. Let others know that you have confidence in them.

Be a learner and a listener. Spend more time gaining wisdom and knowledge than giving it. Be proud of who you are. Your Creator has already affirmed you. He looked on all of His creation and declared it very good.

He takes pride in you.

Dress to succeed.

Success usually comes
to those who are too
busy to be looking for it.

—Henry David Thoreau

APPEARANCE

There's just something about successful people—they look like it. Appearance is no substitute for aptitude, but it will get you an audience. The way you look is initially as important as what you know. Dress to succeed. Work on your appearance.

Dress with style. Leisure suits are parked on the back rack of consignment shops. Leave them there! It only takes a thumb through a catalog or magazine to see what the fashion trends are. You don't have to copy the fringe element. But notice what the businessmen are wearing.

Stay neat and clean. You don't have to buy your clothes in Beverly Hills to look like you've been there. Use your iron. Shine your shoes. Keep your hair trimmed. Shower. Use a breath mint.

Ask for an opinion. You don't have to appear on a reality show to get an evaluation of your appearance. Ask those you respect most. Take some hints from "the stands."

Dress to succeed. What's on your body will affect what's on your mind.

Use anger positively.

Anger is a signal, and
one worth listening to.

—Harriet Lerner

ANGER

Some things should make you mad. Anger has a positive side. When you look at the injustice and injury so prevalent in society, it ought to make your blood boil. Someone needs to come to the defense of the defenseless. That person might as well be you.

Put your anger to positive use. Stand up for someone who has been rejected. You see these kinds of people at work. They live in your neighborhood. You hear their cries. The anger you feel over the injustice served on someone you know has a remedy—your words, your smile, your comfort.

Let your anger be transformed into the motivating force behind your good efforts. Your skills can make a better life for someone. You can build a home for the homeless. You can mentor someone who has been abandoned. You can provide transportation to a social agency for someone who needs its program.

Pick a cause—religious, social, or political. Then do your best to turn wrongs into right.

Don't get even. Just get motivated.

Be a wordsmith.

Good communication is as
stimulating as black coffee and
just as hard to sleep after.

—Anne Morrow Lindbergh

COMMUNICATION

The right words can be a thing of beauty. A silversmith takes raw material and refines, forms, and polishes it into something beautiful. You can do the same with words.

We all have the same raw material to work with—the same alphabet. But those letters can be used either for beauty or for burden. Use them beautifully. Be a wordsmith.

Your entire day is usually built around communication. Whether in the home, on the job, in the classroom, or on the golf course, your words make a difference.

Choose words carefully. Use them as a walking stick rather than a weapon. Choose the helpful over the hurtful. Let someone lean on your words rather than dodge them.

Find some new words. Read through the newspaper. Add a new word to your vocabulary and use it today.

Use words to heal. If you see someone who is hurting, use healing words. "I'm sorry." "Is there anything I can do to help?"

A word to the wise: Use wise words.

Don't be afraid to cry.

No man has the right to dictate what other men should perceive, create or produce, but all should be encouraged to reveal themselves, their perceptions and emotions, and to build confidence in the creative spirit.

—Ansel Adams

EMOTIONS

We're much better at emotions now. In days of old, when a grown man cried he was considered weak. Now, letting your emotions show is often considered a sign of strength.

Face it, we're emotional beings. We get goosebumps when the flag passes. We laugh at corny jokes. We feel our heartbeat quicken when someone crowds into our lane on the entrance ramp to the freeway. We weep when we lose a friend or loved one.

"Where did that feeling come from?" we ask. The answer is simple. It was factory installed. Feelings are not an option, like a DVD player built into a new car. They are a standard feature. Each emotion plays a part in your overall mental and physical health.

So, don't be afraid to laugh. Laughter is a way of relieving tension.

Don't be afraid to cry. Tears are God's way of draining off excess hurt.

Don't be afraid to get angry. Anger is given to preserve safety.

Emotions help you deal with the commotion.

Keep good study habits.

I will study and get ready, and perhaps my chance will come.

—Abraham Lincoln

STUDY

Not long after you took that walk across the graduation platform, you realized that you weren't through with your studies. Study isn't just for those trying to graduate from college. You have a lot to learn, even after you've learned a lot.

Good study habits assist learning. Bad study habits assist burning.

Even football players have to study. Training camp isn't just calisthenics, drills, or T-bone steak dinners in the cafeteria. Each player is expected to spend some time studying plays.

You may not be called to take a lateral from a star quarterback in an NFL game, but life will hand you some things for which you'll need to be prepared.

Study history. You can learn from the past.

Study current events. Stay in the "now," and you'll be in the "know."

Study nature. God's creation is a wonderful classroom.

Study others. Someone you know may already have won the battle you are facing.

Study the Bible. Life has already been mapped out.

Be willing to do the research and study required to do your job with excellence. Be known as someone who may not have all the answers but can be relied upon to find them out.

Don't forget your studies. You still need to pass LIFE 101.

Don't forget others.

Treasure your relationships,
not your possessions.

—Anthony J. D'Angelo

RELATIONSHIPS

Life isn't a one-man show. It's a drama played out with other actors. The way you interact with others will mean the difference in your success or failure.

Take some "acting lessons."

Learn how to play off other people's lines. Words and actions give you a cue as to how you should react. Their trauma calls for your tenderness. Their words of affection call for yours in return. Their anger calls for your calming strength.

Keep from upstaging those around you. Actors are trained to stay out of another's light. They are taught not to stand between their fellow actor and the audience. That's good advice for relationships, too. Let others enjoy the spotlight. Give an opportunity for someone to be seen and get the applause.

Listen for cues. Sometimes actors forget their lines. They depend on their fellow actors to cue them. Relationships are the same way. There are times when you won't know what to say. Listen to the cues of others—their reactions, their tone of voice—and react accordingly.

Life really is a stage. Perform well before the curtain falls.

Admit your faults.

The greatest of faults,
I should say, is to be
conscious of none.

—Thomas Carlyle

FAULTS

You have something that is totally unique: your own faults. Everyone has faults, but they're not like yours. Yours are tailor made. They fit your personality. They may reflect your family tree, your home, or your neighborhood. But they have your name on them.

Never be afraid to admit it when you're wrong. Owning up to your mistakes is more a sign of strength than weakness. Weak men are whiners. Winners are men who can face a fault and turn it into a fortune.

Admit it when you've said the wrong thing. "I'm sorry" is a phrase that has power to change the entire atmosphere in a room. Use it often.

Admit it when you've done the wrong thing. You'll never be perfect in performance, but you can be perfect in purpose. Sometimes your heart will be in the right place, but your hands and your feet will betray you. Fess up.

Faults aren't failures. Sin is a failure. And since Jesus was without sin, He's the only one who can take care of your sins—if you'll ask.

Take batting practice.

Toil to make yourself
remarkable by
some talent or other.

—Seneca

SKILLS

In baseball, the best hitters are those who practice batting. They spend time in the batter's cage, taking swings at pitches. It's the same way in life. Practice doesn't always make you perfect, but it will make you better.

Some skills are natural. Others have to be learned. For example, some baseball players seem to have natural ability. They run faster. They're seemingly more coordinated. They have a better focus. They have natural throwing skills.

Others have to work at it. They're still on the field, while the other players are on their way to the locker room. They spend extra time fielding and running extra laps. They're still playing catch while others are on their way home.

Champions work on their skills. They take what's been given to them and perfect it. They may not win the Golden Glove awards. They may not even wear a championship ring. But they are winners because they are "improvers."

Work on your skills. Do what you can do; only do it better tomorrow than you did it today.

Tell the truth.

Where is there dignity
unless there is honesty?

—Cicero

HONESTY

Your nose won't grow when you tell a lie, but everything else about you will stop growing—your spirit, your character, your resolve. Dishonesty is the first mile down the road to failure.

George Washington said, "I cannot tell a lie." That was when he was young. Later on, he may have abandoned his pledge. Only God knows. But you can tell a lie. You're born with that tendency. It goes all the way back to the Garden of Eden. Your ancestors were fibbers.

You can break the chain. You can determine to be honest in your words, your actions, and your attitudes.

You can pay the entire amount of your income tax—even when others are fudging figures. You can admit to making the decision that ruined that office project. You can confess to that police officer who pulled you over for doing fifty miles per hour in a thirty-five miles per hour speed zone. "You're right, officer. I was doing fifty."

With God's help, you can make honesty your only way of life.

Adjust to change.

Everything changes
but change itself.

—John F. Kennedy

CHANGES

"**S**omething's different," you say as you make your morning commute. "Over there, where that convenience store used to be, there is an empty field. When did that happen? This neighborhood is really changing."

You're right. Not only is the neighborhood changing; the community is changing. In fact, the world is changing. Nothing is the same as it was.

War creates changes.

Scientific achievements change the way we do things.

Technology changes our world.

Men and machines are moving all the familiar landscapes. You can either fight it or go with the flow. The difference will mean not only your sanity but also your success.

Accept change. Admit that it's not all bad. In fact, some change is good—really good. Air conditioning, Novocain, color television, MP3s—each advancement helps you feel, see, hear, or live better. The only thing our changing world can't do is make you act better. You'll have to work on that yourself.

Create change. Some things shouldn't stay the way they are—your roof, your landscape, your golf score, your neighborhood.

You can be an agent of change and a changed agent.

Start a strength-training regimen.

The undertaking of a new action brings new strength.

—Evenius

STRENGTH

Those people doing reps with weights in the gym aren't just working on muscles. They're working on spirit. They're working through their pain for the sake of gain. They know that a disciplined routine will help them reach their personal best.

It's the same in life. A strength-training regimen will help you reach your goals.

Strengthen your attitude. Practice putting off the unkind remarks of others, and accept people for who they are.

Strengthen your character. Learn to say no, even if it's unpopular. Lead instead of following. Deny the moment for the sake of the lifetime.

Strengthen your heart. Fill it with godly thoughts. Memorize God's promises. Mirror His actions. Put others first. Give your quality time to the church, not your leftover time.

Strengthen your bonds. Put your life on the line for the sake of another. Make personal sacrifices for the help or healing of someone you love.

Go for it! Aim for eternity, and you won't miss life.

Wave the flag.

I only regret that I have one
life to lose for my country.

—Nathan Hale

PATRIOTISM

It's your country. God put you here. Through the heroism of men and women throughout time, He gave the liberties that make you free. Don't be afraid to wave the flag. Don't be afraid to be a patriot.

There are people who hate your freedom to walk down a city street when you want to. They hate your free speech. They hate your opportunity to make a living in a career of your choice. They hate those things enough to do everything in their power to destroy them.

Take a stand for your freedom.

Talk like a patriot. Stand up for your country. Commend the deeds that have resulted in your right to say aloud what's on your mind.

Vote like a patriot. There's more power in a vote than in a thousand missiles. But the missiles will prevail if patriots are lazy about voicing their opinions.

Walk like a patriot. Live the principles that formed the framework of our democracy.

You can do it. You must do it!

Seize the moment.

True happiness . . . arises,
in the first place, from the
enjoyment of one's self.

—Joseph Addison

ENJOYMENT

There's something that has the potential to be a precious gem you will cherish forever—the moment. It may be a day, an hour, or a minute. But a moment in time is one of life's greatest treasures.

You'll recognize it. It will have a golden glow about it. You may be with family, friends, or associates; but you'll recognize it as a time that can never be re-lived.

Slow down. Take time to look for the moment. Make room for an opportunity that is filled with faith, friendship, or fun.

Look up. Meditate. Reflect. Read. Pray. Sing. Let your heart drift beyond the horizon of time toward eternity.

Stay alert. It's only a moment. It will be gone before you know it. Children will grow. Spouses will age. Friends will turn to others. This is your moment in time to enjoy completely.

You may only have a moment, but it's all you need to turn a gloomy day into one that is sunny.

And don't forget, God gave it to you; He turned your day into a golden moment.

Love your grandchildren.

Recommend to your children
virtue; that alone can make
them happy, not gold.

—Ludwig Van Beethoven

GRANDCHILDREN

You may not be qualified yet. But someday you might be called to duty. So you'd better practice, just in case. You may be a grandpa.

Some of you have already answered the call. You know what it's like to cherish pictures in a wallet, a walk on the beach, or the push of a swing—to spend time with your grandchildren.

Grandparents (or pre-grandparents) are always in training.

They're learning how to give room to grow. Yesterday's ideas don't fit into today's mold. Today is a new day unlike any other. Grandpas don't have to surrender their *ideals,* but sometimes they have to release their grasp on their *ideas.*

Grandparents are learning how to love. Today's grandchildren are a new edition. They'll do things that would have given a terminal blush in years past. Love accepts people without approving their actions.

Grandparents are learning how to second the motion of parents. Grandparents give better advice from the sidelines than on the playing field. But they're always there if needed.

Love your grandchildren. The dividends are priceless!

Fill your toolbox.

The only use of a knowledge
of the past is to equip
us for the present.

—Alfred North Whitehead

EQUIPPING

It's nice to have tools around when you need them—wrenches, screwdrivers, saw blades, clamps. You'll never know when the right tool will bring about running water, lights, or an opened garage door. The secret is in having the right tools.

There are some tools that will make your life run more efficiently.

Self-control. Handling your emotions opens doors. Nobody wants to invest in someone who acts first and thinks later. If you fly off the handle, you'll probably hit somebody.

Courtesy. Treating others with respect always makes things run smoother. A kind word, a spontaneous good deed, an opened car door—courtesy is irreplaceable.

Spirituality. A heart for God allows light to come in. Like a flashlight shining on a shadowy path, faith helps you find your way and provides a sense of safety.

You'll think of others—tools that you have already used to bring you this far, tools that you may need to add to your toolbox.

Keep your toolbox full, and you'll have what you need to build a successful life.

Light the grill.

Small cheer and great welcome
makes a merry feast.

—William Shakespeare

HOSPITALITY

That place where you live is more than a house or an apartment. It's an oasis. It's a place where people can come to find refreshment. You don't have to throw an extravagant party to lighten someone's spirit. Barbecued spareribs may be all they need. The secret isn't in the food, the beverage, or the price of the grill. The secret is in the attitude of the host.

Don't leave the hospitality to your spouse. Take the lead. Make people feel welcome. They've come from the cold, no matter what the season may be. They've come from a world of numbers. They need a warm handshake, a kind smile, a pleasant word.

Make people feel important. Sure, you have ideas. But just listen. Ask a "starter" question and then just let the other person express an opinion.

Make people feel loved. Let God's concern and compassion flow from you. These travelers have been searching for an oasis like yours. Don't disappoint them.

Be a safety inspector.

It is one of the worst
of errors to suppose that
there is any path for safety
except that of duty.

—William Nevins

SAFETY

Let's face it, everything that once was considered safe is now suspect. We've been "nine-elevened." Our security is on full alert. From a bicycle ride to the convenience store to a flight to Paris, everything is different.

You've been appointed as the Safety Inspector. Your job is to make sure that everyone within your home is protected from the elements and from the enemy.

Watch what you watch. Keep your family safe from the evil empires of immorality. Set some television guidelines. Rent DVDs that are uplifting instead of destructive.

Guard the refrigerator. Foods that are high in fat and carbohydrates can be weapons of mass destruction. Think about your daily diet. Set the food standard. People are not only watching you eat; they're watching what you eat.

Keep a watch over your heart. The enemy has won if he has terrorized you. Keep yourself and your family focused on faith. Take God home from church with you. Let Him have control of every room of your house. Trust Him personally. Trust Him collectively.

It's better to be safe than to be sorry.

Focus on the future.

They say a person needs
just three things to be
truly happy in this world:
Someone to love, something to
do, and something to hope for.

—Tom Bodett

156

HOPE

"**T**omorrow" is more than the title of a song in a Broadway musical. It's a spirit. It's an expectancy that the sun will come out, that shadows will soon fade, that life will be better by and by. One of the best things you can do for yourself, and for your family, is to focus on the future. Hope.

How?

Remember that God has everything under control. From the first dawn to the last sunset, God has been in charge of every event. And He'll continue to be in charge throughout eternity.

Trust Him. Place your confidence in Him. Sign your name to His promises.

Don't focus on your problems. Let someone else think about them. Focus on fixing. Focus on faith. Work on solutions rather than worrying about problems.

Keep singing. A song has a way of running off the "glooms." If you can't sing, whistle. And if you can't whistle, put on your favorite uplifting CD. Turn your situation into a sanctuary of praise.

Approach life with hope for a brighter tomorrow.

Be an overcomer.

We grow because we struggle,
we learn and overcome.

—R. C. Allen

OVERCOMING

Anyone can quit, and many have. Some haven't given up; they've just let up, as in a stock car race where the lead car was ahead by too many seconds. Someone settled for second. The money was still good. They still got some points in the standings.

But winners aren't happy with second place. They'll do everything to overcome obstacles—whether the obstacle is a flat tire, low fuel, or a spin out. The finish line is worth the extra effort. How do the people in Victory Lane overcome adversity?

Focus on the finish. Looking back is dangerous in life and in racing.

Stay alert. From your very first driver's education class, you've been told to "keep your eyes on the road." Focus is just as important in life.

Stay in touch with the Chief Engineer. In racing, the driver is in constant communication with someone who has a better view of the track—who knows the conditions of the car and driver. You have a similar advantage. Your heavenly Father sees everything. He knows the conditions. And He knows you.

Be an overcomer. Don't settle for second when you can be in the victory lane.

"Gentlemen, start your engines!"

About the Author

Dr. Stan A. Toler is general superintendent in the Church of the Nazarene with an office at the Global Ministry Center in Lenexa, Kansas.

He was chosen for the highest elected office in the church at the 27th General Assembly at Orlando, Florida, USA, in July 2009, after serving for 40 years as a pastor in Ohio, Florida, Tennessee, and Oklahoma.

Stan Toler has written over 80 books, including his best-sellers, *God Has Never Failed Me, But He's Sure Scared Me to Death a Few Times; The Buzzards Are Circling, But God's Not Finished With Me Yet; God's Never Late, He's Seldom Early, He's Always Right on Time; The Secret Blend; Richest Person in the World; Practical Guide to Pastoral Ministry; The Inspirational Speaker's Resource, ReThink Your Life*, his popular *Minute Motivator* series, *If Only I Could Relate To The People I'm Related To* and his newest book, *God Can Do Anything But Fail: So Try Para-Gliding In A Windstorm*.

Toler recently was honored with a honorary Doctorate of Divinity from Southern Nazarene University.

He and his wife, Linda, an educator, have two married sons, Seth (Marcy) and Adam (Amanda), and two grandsons Rhett and Davis.

To Contact the Author

Stan Toler
E-mail: stan@stantoler.com
Website: www.StanToler.com

If you have enjoyed this book, or if it has impacted your life, we would like to hear from you.

Please contact us at:
Dust Jacket Press
PO Box 721243
Oklahoma City, OK 73172

Or through our website: www.dustjacket.com